Houses of New Orleans

Alex Caemmerer

4880 Lower Valley Road Atglen, Pennsylvania 19310

Acknowledgments

I would like to thank John Michael Vlach, Professor of American History and Anthropology at George Washington University, Washington, D.C., for his help in making suggestions and offering further information, especially about shotgun houses and their African-Caribbean origins.

I also wish to thank Karen Kingsley, former professor at Tulane University School of Architecture, for her expertise and help in describing the style and architectural details of the individual houses.

I would also like to thank John Magill, Curator/Historian at the Williams Research Center of the Historic New Orleans Collection, for reviewing the text and offering suggestions.

The production of this book has been a collaborative family effort, and I wish to thank the following members of my family for their efforts on this project: my wife, Li Caemmerer, graphic designer and painter, who did the sketching of and art work on the map; my son, William Caemmerer, website designer, who rendered the map for publication; my son John Caemmerer, a Waldorf teacher, who edited the text; and my son, Alex Caemmerer III, computer scientist, who handled the computer technology.

Dedication

I wish to dedicate this book to my three wonderful granddaughters, Margaret, Aurelia, and Carolyn Caemmerer, so they will have something to remember me for besides my chicken gravy and pumpkin pie.

Covers and book designed by Bruce Waters
Type set in Zurich BT

ISBN: 978-0-7643-3117-6

Printed in China

Schiffer Books are available at special discounts for bulk purchases for sales promotions or premiums. Special editions, including personalized covers, corporate imprints, and excerpts can be created in large quantities for special needs. For more information contact the publisher:

Published by Schiffer Publishing Ltd.
4880 Lower Valley Road
Atglen, PA 19310
Phone: (610) 593-1777; Fax: (610) 593-2002
E-mail: Info@schifferbooks.com

For the largest selection of fine reference books on this and related subjects, please visit our web site at **www.schifferbooks.com**
We are always looking for people to write books on new and related subjects. If you have an idea for a book please contact us at the above address.

This book may be purchased from the publisher.
Include $5.00 for shipping.
Please try your bookstore first.
You may write for a free catalog.

In Europe, Schiffer books are distributed by
Bushwood Books
6 Marksbury Ave.
Kew Gardens
Surrey TW9 4JF England
Phone: 44 (0) 20 8392-8585; Fax: 44 (0) 20 8392-9876
E-mail: info@bushwoodbooks.co.uk
Website: www.bushwoodbooks.co.uk
Free postage in the U.K., Europe; air mail at cost.

Contents

Foreword

A book on the historic houses of New Orleans written so soon after the devastation of Hurricanes Katrina and Rita could easily assume the tone of a eulogy given the extraordinary devastation wrought by those killer storms. But Alex Caemmerer has found much in Crescent City that is worthy of celebration. Key sections of the city such as Uptown, the Garden District, the French Quarter, and Bywater were left relatively untouched because, ironically, they were so close to the Mississippi River. For thousands of years, the annual floods of North America's longest river deposited enough soil to raise a natural levee to a height that has protected those structures built close to the river. Caemmerer, strolling through these neighborhoods with his trusty cameras at the ready, has garnered a rich sampling of intriguing residential buildings that collectively provide New Orleans with a distinctive signature of place. These buildings, when joined with the performances of the city's world renowned musicians and chefs, show that the city, while still facing many challenges, remains vibrant at its core.

While many think of New Orleans as a southern city, it is actually a place that is in cultural terms actually south of the South. As far back as the 1720s, the city has had important historical links to the development of the Caribbean islands including Sainte Domingue (now Haiti and the Dominican Republic), Martinique, and Guadeloupe. The city's numerous Creole houses, and its shotgun houses too, all have clear antecedents that can readily be found on these various island domains. West Indian immigrants, who were constantly arriving in New Orleans, when faced with the need to find shelter understandably turned to familiar Caribbean building types. These were structures that typically featured extended eaves, high ceilings, substantial porches or verandas, and large openings closed by tall louvered shutters that might function both as doors and windows. Such houses offered their residents needed relief from the heat and humidity and were much admired by many distinguished visitors including Benjamin Latrobe, architect of the United States Capitol. Before long, American settlers also realized that it was best to follow local traditions whenever possible. The well-known sequence of so-called national styles that arose during the nineteenth century – classical revival, gothic revival, Italianate, second empire and so on – were all amended in some way to fit the cultural style of New Orleans.

In this book, Alex Caemmerer joins forces with thousands of New Orleanians who remain committed both to the preservation of old buildings and the appreciation of the profound and complex history that they represent.

John Michael Vlach
Professor of American Studies and Anthropology, George Washington University Washington, D.C.

Preface

Hurricane Katrina of August, 2005 and the subsequent flooding of the major part of New Orleans will go down as one of the most devastating natural disasters in the history of this country. Had the levees not been breached by the surge out of Lake Ponchartrain, the city could well have survived the hurricane winds, sustaining mostly reparable damage to most residential buildings. But most of the city's neighborhoods are located as low as six feet below sea level in the bowl that contains the City of New Orleans. This pervasive flooding caused either immediate vast devastation of houses or made them unusable and irreparable due to the prolonged drenching and the inevitable development of mold and wood rot. The process of demolition and rebuilding of the neighborhoods involved represents a horrendous task, which will probably require years to complete – if ever.

There is one bright spot in that human and architectural disaster. The central – and original – city of New Orleans comprises the Garden District, the Lower Garden District, Central City, the French Quarter, also known as the Vieux Carre, and the Creole faubourgs, such as the Marigny. These were the original neighborhoods of the city and the first areas to be developed and built upon. Fortunately, the early planners and developers selected the higher ground along the Mississippi for their settlements. And the Mississippi River deposited a lot of soil over the years, forming a natural levee in those areas. Consequently these areas were above the flood waters that engulfed the rest of the city following the failure of the levees. The levees were constructed in order to expand the city limits, but as is now well known, they were engineered and built to withstand no more than a Class 3 hurricane. Katrina was a 5.

Fortunately the virtual architectural museum of historic domestic buildings dating from the early part on the Nineteenth Century to its last decade survived with only limited damage from the high winds. For the most part, such wounds as blown-off roofs, broken windows, or other injuries from fallen trees or flying debris comprise the extent of the storm damage. By six months after Katrina, most of this damage had been repaired or is well into the process in these areas. The only real change in these areas is the absence of the abundant trees that surrounded the houses. Local representatives of organizations interested in the preservation of these houses have expressed pleasant surprise at the rapid return to normalcy in these areas.

The photos in this volume, taken in 1992, are of early workers' homes and, in the Garden District, more upscale residences. They represent the variety of architectural styles as they developed, evolved, and metamorphosed through the various architectural idioms over the last two centuries. It is an architectural legacy like no other in this country.

Introduction

To the interested visitor with an appreciation of Nineteenth Century American architecture, New Orleans offers a veritable feast for the eyes: the Vieux Carre and Creole faubourgs to the north and east, the Lower Garden district stretching away from the Mississippi River, and the extraordinarily lovely Garden District combine to present a seemingly endless array of architectural gems that is perhaps without equal in any other American city.

The history of New Orleans architecture is rich and complicated. To do it proper justice would require something on the order of the so-far seven-volume treatise *New Orleans Architecture*, the monumental project sponsored by the Friends of the Cabildo in conjunction with the Louisiana State Museum. I advise anyone seriously interested in the subject to consult this comprehensive and scholarly book series. In addition to offering an exhaustive history of the city and its architecture, it contains a systematic inventory of hundreds of individually researched houses. This opus was the source of much of the information gathered for the present

volume, and I gratefully acknowledge my indebtedness to its authors. Another highly recommended sourcebook on New Orleans architecture is *Southern Comfort*, by E. Frederick Starr, a monumental work on the culture, the people, the architecture and the architects of the Garden District.

The present volume offers a representative sample of the houses built in Nineteenth Century New Orleans. Of the many hundreds of outstanding architectural specimens, only a very small number could be included. Collected here are some of the most esthetically appealing, photogenic, and authentically restored houses of their type still standing. They give an overall impression of the beauty, dignity, and richness of New Orleans architecture that cannot be conveyed by words alone. But even so, only by walking the streets of this beautiful city can one appreciate the sheer number of intriguing and gorgeous antique houses that have been preserved for all to enjoy. Strolling through the neighborhoods of present-day New Orleans is, without exaggeration, like visiting a colossal, open-air art museum.

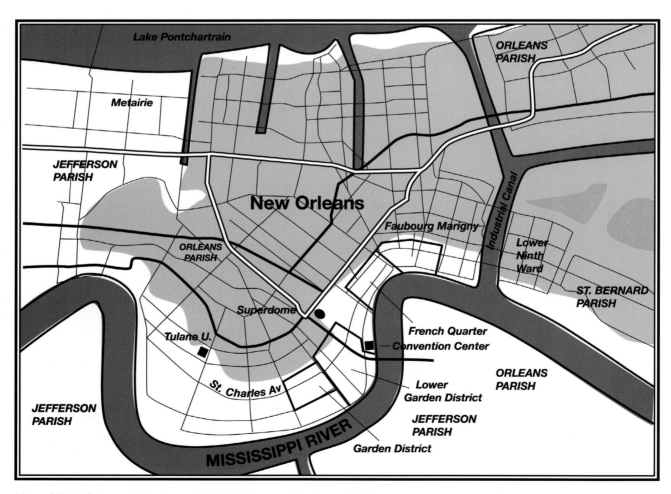

Map of New Orleans, late August, 2005, following Hurricane Katrina, several days after the flooding. Flooded area shown in green.

Historical Background

Although New Orleans was already an important and bustling port in the Eighteenth Century, it was in the 1820s, after the Louisiana purchase of 1803, that the city's greatest period of growth began. It soon became the center of wealth in the south, and it is said that more money could be made there than anywhere else in the country at that time. The area had the country's highest concentration of millionaires, and the great plantations along the Mississippi were being built. The port became the largest in the country, serving the enormous newly-acquired area of the United States to the west of the Mississippi. The necessary workers poured in, too, with many of the new arrivals being Europeans and freemen or "gens de colour libres."

The large influx of workers created a great demand for housing. Many homes were built by individuals and many more by investors and builders catering to the burgeoning rental market. This sparked a building boom throughout the city. As the city was fast becoming a mixing-pot of people, so its architecture became a visible expression of this variety. This, combined with the wide variety of architectural styles already developing during this period throughout the country, made for an especially rich architectural tapestry in New Orleans. With elements of American Federal, French and Spanish Colonial, Creole, Afro-Caribbean, and a variety of European contributions, the city presented a unique blend of both peoples and architecture.

The areas north and east of the original city, including sections of the Vieux Carre, had once been "habitations," or plantations. These were subsequently divided into "faubourgs," or neighborhoods, often named after the owners of the plantations. The land was sold off in small building lots affordable to the working class. It was in these areas that most of the low-cost and rental housing was built: the creole cottages and shotgun houses that survived are some of the smaller homes of present-day New Orleans.

The home builders of the early part of the Nineteenth Century were mostly free blacks and Creole entrepreneurs. Some were professional architects and builders, but houses were designed and constructed for the most part without the assistance of architects. Construction was the traditional occupation of free blacks of the era in New Orleans. Many of the building contracts were by analogy; contracts would often specify that a house be built like another already in existence, which accounts for the similarity between many of the houses in an area. A vernacular architecture evolved from French and Spanish influences. Carpenter-builders were their own architects, and the styles and designs came from their heads and from the house next door or around the corner. Prevailing styles were incorporated into the design, much of which was quite simple, conservative, and uniform. There was not much innovation or originality in the local vernacular architecture; many houses were merely copies of others or copied from books or drawings of other houses.

"Vernacular architecture might well be the architecture of habit. It is the simplest, most straightforward way of building, the result of pragmatism and familiarity, of custom-rooted and oft-times unconscious preference for basic forms and layouts – even on occasion for certain materials and details – that exist independently of passing taste. In the main it is a salient and underlying form of a pronounced and constant feature that distinguishes one folk building type from another, as well as from more sophisticated and ambitious architectural ventures. Overlaying such forms and features may be the ornamental trappings of this or that architectural style, but solidly underneath the primary characteristics remain."[1]

Certainly this holds true for the basic domestic housing built in New Orleans during the Nineteenth Century. Starting in the Eighteenth Century with the basic Creole cottage as well as early shotguns, the design of this simplest housing went through many changes in its evolution over the decades of Nineteenth Century. Many original Creole cottages were replaced later by shotgun houses, and over the years their street façades and decorations of both types mirrored the changing styles and fashions of the times. American architecture only came into its own in the 1830s and 1840s, and there followed a lively progression of widely varying decorative styles. Starting with the most popular architectural style of the period, the Greek Revival (or Classical Revival, as its variant is called), there followed various romantic styles, including the Italianate, Victorian, Second Empire, Gothic Revival, and Folk Victorian – to name the most important.

New Orleans Domestic Architecture

The city is a veritable museum of Nineteenth Century American architecture. The working-class neighborhoods are filled with a variety of modest housing, mostly Creole cottages and shotgun houses, while the upper-income areas developed later in the Nineteenth Century, are composed of mostly larger, two-story Classical Revival townhouses and other Classical Revival house types, as well as a variety of more romantic types, such as Italianate, Victorian, and the like.

The basic plan of the smaller houses remained quite similar over the years, while the street façades were altered and modified. These small houses were frequently renovated, enlarged, redecorated, and even demolished and replaced by a newer building of a more fashionable style. What is left today is an array of small houses in various degrees of restoration representing every period in the evolution of architectural style and taste, both in New Orleans and the rest of the country.

Industrialization brought with it mass-produced ornamentation – millwork, brackets, window and door surrounds, and a whole host of prefabricated ornamental elements that were readily available to the low-income homeowner and were generously applied to these houses. Although modest in size and construction, these houses gradually appropriated many of the decorative elements found on more imposing homes and imitated the look of elegance and good taste. As early as the 1830s, millwork was available from local door and blind factories, and Roberts Catalogue of 1857 had a full line of decorative treatments for purchase. Houses that had begun with a Greek Revival motif often later found themselves trimmed with Victorian ornaments, with shutters and roofs painted in a wide variety of colors. Today these areas contain examples running the full gamut of Nineteenth Century house styles

and decorative elements. The wide variety of house types in New Orleans, some new and some evolving out of earlier designs, all experienced a dressing up from time to time as styles changed and newer building materials and decorative elements became available.

The Lower Garden District and the Creole faubourgs comprise the working-class area of New Orleans and contain the more modest dwellings: the one and two-level side-hall townhouses, the center hall cottage, the villa, and the shotgun, the most common house type in this area, Of these Nineteenth Century house types, the most colorful and unique were the Creole cottages and the ubiquitous shotgun houses. However, over the years, most Creole cottages have either been altered to resemble or been replaced by shotgun houses. These two types are especially well represented in the present collection, and in the descriptions that follow of the various house styles, these two types receive special attention.

Quite characteristic of New Orleans houses, large and small, and part of the elegance of their design were the ever-present, generous, shaded galleries, high ceilings and spacious rooms. Ventilation was of prime concern in those days.

What impresses one most about the architecture of the houses of New Orleans is the beauty and dignity of design of even the most modest dwellings. At the same time, one cannot help but be amazed at the sheer number and quality of examples concentrated in one city; walking through the neighborhoods, one realizes that nearly all of the houses are positively beautiful, if not downright stunning. It is hoped that this brief history and description of the architectural styles of the houses of New Orleans will help the reader enjoy and appreciate more fully the photographs gathered in this collection.

Early House Types

There are a wide variety of New Orleans houses, from the Early French Colonial plantation prototypes of the Eighteenth Century, to the ubiquitous shotgun houses and the romantic styles of the second half of the Nineteenth Century. The early indigenous houses can be divided into twelve different types.

The French Colonial Plantation House, in its earliest prototypes, was characterized by its steeply pitched hip roof, which was double pitched or canted and "turned up sharply" at the eaves, covering the galleries. It had dormers on all four sides with fluted, capped pilasters and round arch lights. It was usually raised above ground and of *brique entre poteaux* ("brick between post") construction. A majestic and beautiful example of this type is the recently restored Destrehan Plantation House just north of New Orleans.

The Manor House was similar to the French Colonial Plantation House but on a smaller scale, appearing in the city limits from the 1820s on. It was more of a family-sized house than the larger plantation homes.

The Louisiana Plantation House was the commonest type of large plantation dwelling and could be found throughout Louisiana. Although the style was much like the French Colonial, the floor plan was more like the 1820s Greek Revival, with its typical center hall with two or three rooms on either side. There are many in existence today in various states of restoration. A drive up the Mississippi to Natchez offers a sampling of these magnificent structures to the interested tourist.

Creole House Types

Creole houses or cottages of various types were the commonest early domestic housing in the city and comprised a major portion of New Orleans working class homes. They came in a variety of sizes, styles, and degrees of luxury, including the utter lack thereof. These include the ubiquitous cottages with their street façades of varying widths, as well as one and two storytownhouses, also with façades of different widths and designs. Their chief distinguishing features were the gable-sided roof with dormers and the four-rooms-in-a-square floor plan with central chimney. The very earliest, primitive Creole houses were gone by the 1820s.

One can distinguish ten stages in the development of Creole cottages from a former plantation city subdivision. The room arrangement, the presence or absence of galleries, whether set *at the banquette* or back on the lot, whether hip-roofed or side-gabled or a combination of the two, whether there is a garden or kitchen. These are some of the elements used in describing the variants of the Creole cottage.

The four-bay, gable-sided Creole cottage was the most prevalent early house type in the Creole suburbs. It had four large rooms arranged in a square with a gallery to the rear and cabinets (storage rooms) on each side. The earlier ones were usually made of brick-between-post or plastered brick. There was no front gallery, but an *abat-vent* overhang was usually present. Some had hip roofs. The later ones were constructed in a slightly unusual manner using *madriers debouts* or standing planks. These heavy flat planks stood vertically on the sills that were covered with horizontal weatherboards.

Destrahan Plantation is one of the few surviving New Orleans plantations. Located several miles above New Orleans, it was built by Robert Antoine Robin de Longy over a period of three years, 1787-1790. He died in 1792 enjoying it for only a short time. It was acquired in 1802 by Jean Noel Destrehan, his son-in-law, for whom it was named. He was a prominent politcal figure in Louisiana at the time. It is in the West Indies style, with additions on either side to accommodate his large family. It was renovated in 1839 when acquired by another son-in-law of Jean Destrehan, who changed the style to the more popular Greek Revival. The earlier collonettes were covered with brick and plaster to form the existing white columns. After many years of neglect, the house was donated to the River Road Historical Society, which proceeded to restore the manor house and several acres of grounds. It is typical of the early plantations houses surrounding New Orleans before many were sold off during the early part of the nineteenth century and sub-divided into building lots for low-income worker housing. These faubourgs, or neighborhoods, were often named after the plantation.

Most four-bay Creole cottages are about 28 feet wide and 40 feet deep, with a rear gallery and courtyard, and usually a kitchen building and kitchen garden beyond that. Both the front and the rear roofs usually have double dormers, with chimneys between, serving four fireplaces. A number of these houses were built with front galleries; these are referred to as *maison principales.* Four-bay Creole cottages display a wide variety of ornamentation and many variations, including foundation ventilators, boxed-step enclosures, variable door panels, *abat-vent*, or overhang treatment, various pediments, panel patterns on shutters and doors, and various window and door surrounds. Colors are varied and often quite bright and striking, including Paris green, yellow ochre, oxblood red, salmon, blue, and aqua. Seeing this variety of colors today, one wonders whether they are contemporary designer hues, but research has confirmed their authenticity.

This double Creole cottage is reminiscent of the style first seen in the early part of the nineteenth century in New Orleans, as there are no signs of the later Italianate, Victorian, classic, or Greek revival motifs, The gable sided roof is double-pitched at the eaves to incorporate the overhang, typical of the original Creole cottages.

This is perhaps the best example one can find in New Orleans of a double Creole cottage with dormers of the type dating back to the early part of the nineteenth century. Parapets frame the gable-ended roof. The six-over-six lights in the dormers are typically very early. The decorative cornices over the doors and windows and brackets under the overhang are in the Italianate style, and therefore were probably added at a later date when that style became popular. It is truly an elegant example of the typical and distinctive early domestic architecture found only in New Orleans.

The street façade usually presents four evenly spaced openings of four tall doors with casement openings of *deux battans*— glass panels above and solid below. In some cases there are two tall doors and two shorter windows, or alternating doors and windows. Most also have either solid or louvered full-length shutters. Many of these houses were updated later in the Nineteenth Century with various decorative details as new styles became available. One sees numerous examples of what are now described as Victorian cottages, with intricately carved, millwork decorations on what were once typical, plain Creole cottages. The earlier cottages had simple, narrow door surrounds; these later gave way to elaborate and even Italianate entrances. Both front rooms opened on to the street through French doors covered by vertical, boarded shutters.

As people became more affluent and demanded grander homes, this simple house type evolved through more elaborate modifications into larger, four-bay gable-sided houses with front galleries. Later still came the five-bay center hall villas. (Many of the more elegant raised cottages of the Americanized Garden District are variations on these older types. The older, simple designs of both the Creole cottages and the later shotguns strongly influenced the design of many of the more modest Garden District houses)

Other forms of the Creole cottage include the "common-wall" cottages, consisting of two attached double-bay houses. The "dog-trot" house has a narrow alley running between two attached houses.

The two-bay Creole cottage is a relatively rare bird in New Orleans architecture, but the ones remaining are extraordinarily charming and unique.

With one room behind the other and "cabinet" and gallery in the rear, they are appealing and picturesque because of their unusual high-pitched roof design. Those with hip roofs were referred to as *maisonettes* to distinguish them from those with gable-sided roofs. There were usually two full-length openings on the façade, typically in the Greek Revival style. These houses were second generation replacements of the original Creole two-room, hip-roofed cabins built on the original lots in a plantation subdivision. Most of the original primitive structures were gone by 1820.

The three-bay Creole cottage came later, in the Greek Revival period (1845-1860), and showed a stronger American influence. They had three front openings, gabled sides and a side entry or hall onto which the rooms opened. The result was a more private residence, corresponding to the higher standard of living of its owner. Its innovative design was not appreciated by some, who felt it to be a "detestable lop-sided London house," in which a common passage and stairs acts as a common sewer to all the necessities of the dwelling and renders it impossible to preserve a temperature within the house."[2] Nowadays they are seen not only in the Creole areas, but with much more sophisticated and American style façades in the elegant Garden District. The floor plan and general design was appropriated and developed into a more Classical Revival style and motif. The latter, three-bay version of the Creole cottage, with a full-length Greek key entrance and two short, double-hung windows, represented an Anglo-American influence. It seems to have been the precursor of the shotgun house, according to one group of architectural historians. Certainly the three-bay hip roofed Creole cottage strongly resembles the shotgun house, and many feel that the former was in fact the origin of the latter.

The five-bay center hall house, usually one and a half stories high, was the most common American house type in Louisiana. The floor plan, with a center hall running straight through and one room on either side, provided good ventilation, making it well suited to the climate of New Orleans. Usually of Greek Revival design, these homes had columned galleries and dormers front and rear. Referred to as "American cottages," they, too, were frequently treated to a wide variety of elaborate decorations as the century progressed.

Victorian Creole cottages, the latter-day version of the older Creole cottages, appeared late in the Nineteenth Century. As shotguns became the style of choice in the city, the later Creole cottages were more likely to have Italianate, Classic, or Victorian façades and decorations, though the gable-sided roof of the older Creole houses remained.

Three-bay Creole townhouses had from one to four stories and were usually galleried on the second floor. There were usually attic windows or dormers. The three bay resembles the American townhouse, having similar openings in the façade, the same typical galleries, and similar room arrangements. As in the American townhouses, one finds variants with side or center hallway, one or two stories, with or without galleries, and decorated in either classic or Italianate style.

Four-bay Creole townhouses usually have two stories. This style was found only in the Marigny and was a gable-sided, four-bay double with a balcony or gallery on the second level. It is a variant of the Creole cottage.

Two-bay Creole townhouses, found throughout the city, were a two level, two bay variety with either gable-sided or hip roof, sometimes said to be a cut down version of the three bay.

The Porte-Cochere design dates from the 1830s and is referred to as a "carriageway house." It can have two, three, or four stories with a carriage entrance on the ground level leading to an inner courtyard. It is one of the most common multi-level houses in the Vieux Carre.

Later House Types

Shotgun Houses

The Shotgun House, the most common local housing style in New Orleans, comprised a large portion of working-class homes in the city. Although there is evidence that some shotgun houses were built earlier in some areas of New Orleans, most appeared later than the Creole houses, and in many cases were their replacements as the latter aged and as tastes, fashions, and the population changed in the city. Shotgun houses also came in various sizes and styles and were embellished with elements representing nearly all the architectural styles that appeared in Nineteenth Century America.

New Orleans is considered the home of the shotgun house, and the style is often referred to as the Louisiana shotgun house. Shotgun houses were known in New Orleans in some areas as early as the late Eighteenth and early Nineteenth centuries, but were not widespread until the 1840s when they were mostly of Greek Revival design. The style is thought to have originated at a time when there were an increasing number of free persons of color in New Orleans looking for housing. Although these people were gainfully employed and could afford homes, they were not fully enfranchised until after the Civil War. This meant that they were limited to those areas of the city in which there was only minimal housing. The early shotgun houses in New Orleans were referred to as houses of the *homme de couleur libre* (freeman of color). The Haitians of the city called them *maisons baisses* (low houses). The city was full of these simple houses and they constituted the largest segment of housing for the working population. Early in the Nineteenth Century, when many Blacks from Haiti migrated to New Orleans, the shotgun style began to be more in evidence as it did again from the 1870s through the 1890s, when all of New Orleans experienced a great construction boom.

An elegant five-bay center hall cottage with modest Italianate window and recessed door treatment, includes fluted pilasters, bracketed overhang, and corner quoins, all done in quiet good taste. It is a gem of its type.

Shotgun houses were either custom built by individual carpenters or assembled as "prefabs." In 1880, one company's Product Catalogue listed over 700 manufactured items, including mouldings, handrails, newel-posts, dormers, doors, eaves brackets, balusters, etc., and at least three complete shotgun houses: a single and two doubles, complete with ornate combinations of cornices and moldings. New Orleans became the center for the style, and it spread throughout the South in both rural and urban areas. The wide variety of decorative elaborations is only found in New Orleans, collectively representing every known architectural stylistic variation. By the late Nineteenth Century, shotgun houses were found in almost every rural southern town, mostly in Black neighborhoods. As newly-enfranchised Blacks became able to own homes, it was the usual dwelling in both urban and rural areas.[3] In New Orleans, shotguns ranged in width from two-bay to six-bay, the most frequent being the double shotgun — two two-bay houses with a common wall. Many of these were opened up later to make a single-family dwelling.

The two-bay shotgun house is the simplest of the shotgun variety, and purists among architectural historians feel that it is the only example to which the term should be applied. It is characterized by two openings on the façade, a hall-less entrance and a Greek Key door surround. It can have two French doors or else one door and one shorter window. The interior has at least three rooms, one behind the other. The Creole cottages usually have only two rooms, one behind the other, and it is believed by some that when these cottages were enlarged and rebuilt they were made into shotgun houses.

Dignified hip-roofed, two-bay shotgun house with fleur-de-lis border on cornice and Italianate entablature over door and window. Corner quoins are distinctive in a shotgun house.

A simple three-bay shotgun house with bracketed overhang and no other decorations.

This four-bay classic revival shotgun features simple box gallery pillars and very little decoration. It's in the Creole faubourg area, where it may have started out as a double shotgun, as many of this configuration have. The oval openings in the base are vents.

The three-bay single shotgun house is a more spacious house than the two-bay or four-bay double. It is built with an interior hallway or an entrance leading to a full side gallery serving as a passageway between rooms.[4] It is characterized by three full-height openings or two short windows and one full-height opening. It is considered a more private dwelling, having a hallway through to the rear with rooms opening on to it. This floor plan is more like that of the American townhouse, and such living quarters were associated with a higher standard of living. Later they even sported front galleries, which were not found in earlier Creole cottages.

The four-bay double shotgun house is probably the most common variety of shotgun house in New Orleans. It consists of two single shotguns with a common wall, making four openings on the front façade. There can be any combination of French doors and shorter windows on the façade, but the most common consists of two doors and two windows. Each door opens into a room behind which there are one or more rooms. When such houses were converted to single-family residences it left two front rooms without any hallway to the rear rooms. A very common example of this variety of shotgun is now seen in the Victorian

double shotgun house, which usually has a front gallery decorated with elaborate Victorian millwork in friezes, balustrades, moldings, etc. It is not difficult to imagine that many of these double shotguns were derived from or had originally been Creole cottages, and many experts feel that this was, in fact, their origin.

New Orleans shotguns built before the mid-Nineteenth Century were decorated in the Greek Revival style, whereas after that time many were decorated mostly in Victorian, Queen Anne, Italianate, or Second Empire styles with great individuality and sophistication, including complicated detailing in the millwork and window and door treatments. The doors were pilastered and recessed, the windows had cap-molded lintels, and there was usually a front gallery rather than an overhang porch. There is no end to the variety of elaborately decorative styles represented in New Orleans shotgun houses.

Later on, Louisville, Kentucky, and other cities became centers of proliferation of the shotgun style. Even Miami, Florida, had, until recently, a large area built up mostly of Southern shotgun houses. As land values have increased in cities, this kind of housing has been largely replaced, whereas in Louisville, Kentucky, their preservation and restoration is said to have become almost an obsession.

Origins of the Shotgun House

Shotgun houses began to show up late in the Eighteenth Century and early in the eighteenth century when free blacks from Haiti began to arrive. However, they really proliferated in the mid-Nineteenth Century with the increasing influx of Haitians to the city. The area of highest concentration of this type of housing was the lower Mississippi Valley, especially New Orleans and its environs, as well as southern Mississippi and Alabama.[5] According to John Michael Vlach, Professor of American Studies and Anthropology, George Washington University, the shotgun house originated in clustered villages in Africa and was brought first to Haiti by slaves and then to Louisiana when they migrated as freemen to the area. There were two phases of slave trading. The first Africans were captured along the Guinea Coast, (in what is now Nigeria and Daomay) and the second brought in people from Central Africa (Congo and Angola). His description of the shotgun seems to be the accepted one, although there are differences of opinion among architectural historians as to their description and origin.

Some knowledgeable writers on the subject believe that the predecessor of the shotgun house in New Orleans was probably the Creole cottage, a very popular two-bay, hip-roofed, rectangular structure with the narrow end facing the street. It was the most popular minimal housing style in the areas originally inhabited by Creoles and later by freemen in the Eighteenth and early Nineteenth centuries. As these houses deteriorated, they were usually replaced by shotguns. They see no reason to call upon complicated theories of their African and Haitian origins, arguing that:

> The similarity of size, roof, and construction between the Greek revival shotgun and the single creole cottage or maisonette prompts the theory that the shotgun may be an outgrowth of the creole single dwelling type. It is characterized by two façade openings, the hall-less entrance, usually with a Greek key surround, and one short window. Like some creole cottages, there are 2-bay shotguns extending three rooms or more in depth. It is in effect the number of rooms beyond two and the resultant lowering of the pitch of the roof which has caused the differentiation between the creole maisonette and the 2 bay shotgun of obscure origins. [6]

There are a number of theories of the origin of shotgun houses, but Vlach's is the most interesting and convincing. His definition, although not universally accepted among architectural historians, is that:

> . . . the shotgun house is a one-room wide, one-story high building with two or more rooms, oriented perpendicular to the street with its front door on the gable end. These are the essential features of the shotgun house; they are found in all examples. Other aspects – such as size, proportion, roofing, porches, appendages, foundations, trim, and decoration – have been so variable that the shotgun is sometimes difficult to identify. The most important variation in the shotgun is the number of rooms. There can be two to eight or even more. The commonest is three. A notable and distinguishing feature is the placement of the front door. The usual folk house has the door on the long side of the house which is parallel to the street.[5]

Vlach wrote his doctoral thesis on the origin of the Louisiana shotgun house and the influence of cultural and sociological factors on housing styles and patterns. Noting that many of the New Orleans shotgun houses were owned and occupied by people of Haitian origin, he theorized that they had brought their house styles with them from Haiti.

> The shotgun house seems to have developed in New Orleans about the same time that there is a massive infusion of free Blacks from Haiti into the city. The origins of the shotgun are not to be found in the swamps and bayous of Louisiana but on the island of Haiti.[5]

His field study in Porte-au-Prince, where most of the houses are shotguns, revealed that their dimensions – square footage and wall height, for instance – were almost identical to those in New Orleans. He concluded that "it is evident that the shotgun house form was imported from Haiti and with the idea of that form came a host of practices that Haitians considered appropriate and fitting for the type."

Such features as the internal patterning of the rooms, the open bays in the front façade, the extra door in the second room, the arrangement of louvers and shutters, were all a reflection of their particular way of life. Vlach concluded that "the construction of such secondary features in Louisiana clearly showed that Haiti provided the basic model for New Orleans' own shotgun culture."

Vlach traces the large influx of slaves from West Africa to Haiti – first in 1510, and then to an even greater extent from 1730 to 1790, particularly from an area of Nigeria inhabited by the Yoruba people. Although the most common types of houses of these peoples in Africa were made of different materials, such as wattle and daub, thatching, and clay on raffia matting, their homes were rectangular, gable-roofed houses usually of two rooms, one behind the other, and had almost the exact dimensions of the usual Haitian house: 10 feet by 20 feet in Nigeria, and 10 feet by 21 feet in Haiti, with walls between 6 to 8 feet high. Furthermore, the community housing compounds in Africa, the layout of their villages, was almost exactly duplicated in the slave quarters on the plantations of Haiti. All they did in transporting the house to Haiti, Vlach asserts, was to "change a doorway and add a porch."

He further notes "a similar philosophy of space, a culturally determined sense of dimension -- these perceptions of space are used to fix walls and ceilings at appropriate distances." He quotes Amos Rapoport as saying,

> What finally decides the form of a dwelling, moulds the spaces and their relationships, is the vision that people have of the ideal life - the forms of primitive and vernacular buildings are less the result of individual desires than of the aims and desires of the unified group for an ideal environment. Housing therefore reflects the habits and behavior of a culture. The shotgun houses of the Southern blacks afforded a sense of community and intimacy and became one of the most common house forms in all Louisiana. [5]

Vlach concludes that "shotgun houses allowed some important African values to be maintained without extensive modifications, thus helped slaves and later free blacks, endure dreadful social conditions. The shotgun house brought them closer to a life they had lost forever and helped them create a life they preferred. The lesson learned from the case of the shotgun house indicates that, even in areas thought to have the least potential for the survival of Africanism, the African background is present. [The shotgun house] was a culturally determined manifestation of their philosophy of life and an attempt to recreate their original environment in the new lands." [5]

Compared to other theories, that the shotgun house descended from American Indian dwellings, or from the houses of the Louisiana Bayou oystermen, or from the camp houses and boathouses of Mississippi fishermen, or from the Creole cottages of New Orleans, Vlach's is much more complex and sophisticated. Many historians believe that one of these simpler explanations is probably correct. They argue that if the design of the shotgun is so simple and obvious (How many shapes can such a small house have?) then why must it have such a convoluted history?

This objection notwithstanding, Vlach's ideas are intriguing, and his theory convincing. It makes sense that people, as they arrive in a strange new land, would naturally tend to build houses in which they feel at home. Although some groups do not feel the need to duplicate their native architecture in a new land, Vlach

believed that these particular immigrants recreated their home environment in an attempt to relieve the unusual stresses of their new lives. He has said recently, with authority, that the denial of African connections via the Caribbean can no longer stand. Most of American architecture has its origins on the continent of Europe. These observations suggest that the shotgun houses of the South are of distinctly African origin.

As one moves from the Creole faubourgs to the other side of Canal Street, the Lower Garden District, and, finally, to the elegant Garden District itself, one encounters a different collection of architectural styles of later origins. This area of New Orleans was mostly undeveloped open space in the first two decades of the Nineteenth Century. After the Louisiana Purchase, as was already mentioned, there was a building boom. It was in this part of the city that newcomers of other ethnic origins looked to build their homes. A large influx of Irish settled in what is now the Lower Garden District, and part of it is often referred to as the Irish Channel. Other Europeans, including Germans and Italians, added to the city's ethnic mix. Affluent immigrants to the city tended to congregate in an area of their own. It was the Garden District that attracted the newly arriving groups, and it is here that they built their elaborate homes in a variety of styles, often reflecting their national origins. The predominant motif in architecture was the Greek Revival style already popular across the nation. The modified versions of this style are often referred to as Classical Revival.

A simple, ordinary double shotgun of the Creole faubourg features decorative millwork on the eaves, fish scale shingles in the gable, and a bracketed overhang, like hundreds of others, circa late nineteenth century.

This busy Victorian double shotgun's configuration is perhaps the most common of New Orleans shotgun houses. Many have been opened up and made into single family homes. In this example, the openings are narrow and square-headed. The banded millwork, turned balusters, and collonettes are typically Victorian. Pre-cut millwork decorations were readily available later in the nineteenth century and owners could design their own facades for individuality. The gable front with stained glass windows dates this house to the 1890s or early twentieth century.

Greek Revival Style Houses

The Greek Revival period in American architecture lasted from about 1820 to the Civil War and was the first period in which professional architects became influential. In 1818 William Strickland, one of the earliest American architects of note, introduced the Greek temple style in several public buildings, most notably the Second National Bank of Philadelphia. It was based on the Parthenon in Athens, dating from the Fifth Century B.C. and one of the finest examples of classic Greek architecture. Thomas Jefferson had used this design earlier for the Virginia state capitol, modifying it to suit the American need for inexpensive and rapid construction using locally available materials.

The style became very popular in Louisiana and along the Mississippi River as wealthy landowners started building their plantation homes. They began vying with each other to see who could have the largest and most impressive Greek Temple style mansion. These enormous "mini-Parthenons" were often surrounded on all four sides by fluted Greek columns that exuded power and prestige.

The Greek Revival style also gained popularity in the design of more modest houses in other areas of the country, including Key West, Florida, nearly paralleling the new style in New Orleans. What soon developed was

"A simple rectangular block of more than one storey. It has a low-pitched roof, the main entrance is on the gabled end. The attic story expends beyond the vertical plane of the principal stories, forming a portico. Formal columns (Doric, Ionic, Corinthian, and Tuscan) are an integral part of the portico structure. Square (box) pillars are often substituted for columns and crowned with a few simple moldings instead of classical capitals, A plain frieze of smooth boards and boxed cornice with a few molding strips form a partial entablature. Typically, there is no architrave. A series of small blocks nailed to the soffit board – the board covering the underside of rafters of an overhanging eave – serve as dentils.[7]

Key West, Florida, embraced the Greek Revival style as eagerly as did New Orleans. (It is also, like New Orleans, home to a great many shotgun houses.) There were certain differences, however, in the way the Greek Revival style was applied in the local architecture of the two cities. In Key West the townhouses had a pitched roof forming an attic with front gable facing the street. There was little or no entablature as in New Orleans' townhouses, but instead, usually a simple band as cornice and very few decorations beyond modest brackets or spandrels. Key West had neither the great wealth nor architectural sophistication – nor architects – as in New Orleans. Consequently there was very little of the ornate Italianate or elaborate Victorian decorations. The popular decorations in Key West, often referred to as "gingerbread" and classified in the literature as "Folk Victorian," were quite simple and modest. This is a good example of how different local cultures influence domestic architecture. The flamboyancy and gaiety of New Orleans shows up in the city's architectural preferences, making its style much more decorative, innovative, and playful than almost anywhere else.

The Parthenon, on the Acropolis, Athens, Greece. Built in the fifth century, B.C., it was commisioned by Pericles and designed by architects Ictinus and Callicrates. It represents the pinnacle of great Greek temple architecture in the doric style. In the sixth century it became a Christian church and remained so until 1458, when it became a mosque. It remained intact until 1687, when, under attack by the Venetians, the gunpowder stored there ignited and it was almost completely ruined. It is presently under restoration.

Greek revival double galleried townhouse with split fluted Greek columns with Corinthian capitals up and Doric down. Beautiful recessed door entablature with fluted pilasters, cornice, architrave and pediment. It has many brothers and sisters in the lower garden district.

This front door flaunts an impressive arched, pilastered, corniced, and pedimented surround, exuding elegance and high style.

The double galleried townhouse became very popular in the design of private homes in downtown New Orleans, with Greek columns being placed where ever they might fit in. There were two sources of this style: the plan of the side-halled English townhouse, brought to New Orleans by architects from England, and other townhouse plans brought by architects from New York and Boston. As a result, the Greek Revival, two-level galleried townhouse became the style of choice for in-town houses in New Orleans.

Both the double-galleried side-hall English townhouse and the townhouses of the Northeast were well-suited to modification in the Greek Revival style through the addition of double galleries to the front of the house. Distinctive roof lines were added, from single cornices to elaborate entablatures – including cornice, architrave, and frieze – along with decorations such as dentils and modillions. As the newer styles arrived, brackets in the Italianate style and Victorian decorations were added. Greek columns, either split or full-height, supported the galleries and were topped with Ionic, Doric, and Corinthian capitals. While more elegant homes sported fluted columns and classic capitals, more modest ones had square (box) pillars, usually with Doric capitals. In downtown New Orleans there were blocks upon blocks of these double-galleried side-hall townhouses, making for a very impressive scene.

There were a few raised villa types, a few brick row houses, some few cottages. The most consistent conspicuous visual theme that weaves through the entire area is the galleried housefront with its repetitive grid of post-and-lintel system, more often on two levels. Somehow an idiom came into existence, partly from influences elsewhere in this country, partly through the demands of climate, local custom, and of a reasonable conformity of street aspect. [8]

The plantation type center hall raised cottage, also known as the plantation type villa, is a popular Garden District house type usually done in Greek Revival or Classical Revival style. It is usually generously proportioned and done in either a plain Classical Revival style or more elegantly outfitted with all the most impressive Greek Revival additions and decorations. Included were elaborate roof entablatures, window and door surrounds, and detailed door surround entablatures, including cornices, pilasters, side lights, and transoms.

The five-bay center hall raised cottage, also known as the American cottage, is another popular Lower Garden District and Garden District house type. It is said to be American architecture's contribution to New Orleans architecture. It has one-and-a-half stories, with a spacious first floor gallery and dormers. It is usually done with basic Greek Revival elements, along with Italianate and Victorian decorations.

New Orleans' Vernacular Ornamentation

Since most of these buildings were constructed without the aid of professional architects, they showed individual variations in spite of the general similarity from one house to the next. New Orleans style and individuality showed up in the decorations. The elaborate plaster work, millwork, and cast iron decorations are what make the New Orleans style distinct from other parts of the country. This is the vernacular style now popularly recognized as belonging to New Orleans.

In these buildings the Greek Revival idiom was used loosely and freely and with great charm and individuality seen nowhere else in the country. Ornamental details ran the gamut and included such designs as palmette, honeycomb, anthemionas crest (acroterion), acanthus leaf, bead-and-reed, and egg-and dart motifs, along with the ubiquitous dentils of various size, perhaps the most common decoration on any classic building. Traditional and typically elaborate window and door surrounds also serve to identify the Greek Revival influence. Doors are usually paneled and surrounded on the sides and top by a narrow band of rectangular glass panes.

Cast iron decorations came into general use in the Lower Garden district around 1849, imported from Philadelphia and New York and represent most of what is seen now in New Orleans. However, within a year or so foundries were established in Mississippi to supply capitals, railings, fences, and various supports that were often used to replace wooden decorations. Patterns were varied and abundant. Certainly the wide use of these elaborate and distinctive ironwork decorations on its houses has given New Orleans' architecture a unique and immediately recognizable look, quite different from anywhere else in the country.

While fashionable curlicues were being imported from Paris by the elite, millwork manufacturers were turning out a whole carnival-esque frenzy of scrolled brackets and beaded screenwork or colonnettes turned on a lathe. As in the case of ornamental cast iron, other cities experimented in the genre but only in New Orleans was the popular fancy carried away in a footloose fling of jigsaw whimsy. The high jigsaw movement, in its Moorish, Gothicized, Baroquesque of you-name-it versions, was applied on cottages or two-level galleried singles or doubles – all the various types and schemes that had prevailed in the antebellum phase.[10]

A typical five-bay Louisiana raised cottage with unfluted columns topped by Corinthian capitals. A unique heavy cornice is sectioned and centered by an unusual carved arched pediment. Double pilastered dormers contribute to the many variations one sees in this popular house design.

A Greek revival center hall raised cottage is typical of many in New Orleans, with fluted columns and Corinthian capitals. Low window dormers in the background flank the double arched windows. The cornice is modestly bracketed and arched segmental openings adorn Italianate window and door treatments. The door is recessed behind a pilastered entablature topped with a dentiled cornice. This is a very common style in the Lower Garden District, the Garden District, and throughout Louisiana, and is often referred to as a Louisiana Cottage. This is a particularly good example of this genre.

The Romantic Styles

The Greek Revival style remained popular in New Orleans up to the end of the eighteenth century, long after it had lost popularity in the rest of the country, where it was supplanted by more romantic styles such as Victorian, Queen Anne, Italianate, Second Empire, and Eastlake. But as time passed, these new styles eventually arrived in New Orleans also, not only in design of newly constructed houses, but also in the Victorian and Italianate decorations added to many existing homes. Italianate elements in particular appeared in everything from modest shotgun houses to the most pretentious mansions, with equally impressive effect.

Italianate style houses, inspired by Italian Renaissance architecture, were distinguished by their low roofs with paired brackets in the entablature supporting the wide over-hang. Italianate door and window surrounds were capped with elaborate cornices and pediments – often bracketed – behind segmental arches. Brackets became very popular and frequently appeared in the entablature of Greek Revival houses as they were remodeled. Recessed doors were surrounded by deep cornices and paneled pilasters. Corner quoins were an Italianate feature. Italianate houses often had decorative parapets and turrets, and these additions began to appear all over town; "in New Orleans a building had to have one of these things."[9]

Italianate houses were very ornate and appealed to architects as well as the homeowners of New Orleans. It was the style of choice for remodeling houses in the Garden District; the most popular combination of styles was that of Italianate elements and decorations on a Greek Revival House. The Italianate style dominated New Orleans architecture in the 1860s and 1870s.

Victorian and Queen Anne style houses were distinguished by their asymmetry, multiple vertical planes, facets, and siding, as well as bulging bay-windows and sprouting towers and turrets. The typical Victorian decorative elements that gradually appeared on New Orleans houses of all dimensions were varieties of millwork on porches and galleries: spandrels, open-work friezes (spindle bands) and turned colonnettes. Jig-sawed verge boards also appeared under the eaves of multiple gables. Victorian houses usually had many gables that were variously decorated with sunburst motifs, fish scale shingles, and more. Many of these items were manufactured and readily available for quick application to existing houses as fashion dictated.

Second Empire, another popular style of the period, influenced New Orleans architecture less than others. However, examples of one element of this style—the mansard roof—can be seen both in this area and across town on Esplanade road.

Eastlake was a sort of over-done Victorian style that appeared late in the Victorian period. An English architect, Charles Eastlake, wrote a book on furniture design called Hints on Household Taste in 1872. It became very popular and was the inspiration for a great deal of architectural detailing and millwork. Eastlake himself apparently considered this development extravagant and bizarre and came to regret that his name was associated with it. It was characterized by superfluous gables elaborately decorated with a variety of motifs such as sunbursts, fantails, etc. The houses also sprouted rooster comb finials, jigsaw cresting over window surrounds, lots of open work and piece work bands, turned colonnettes – all extremely intricate. These houses are usually described as Victorian, but they do have distinctive elements inspired by Eastlake.

One of the few two-bay shotgun houses in the Garden District, this gem is dressed for the occasion. The wide overhang is supported by elaborate brackets and decorated with dentate millwork. Simple classic revival cornice and frieze combine to make this a most appealing facade.

Simple two-bay shotgun house with very few decorative elements, typical of those in the Creole faubourgs.

Two-bay camelback shotgun house with bracketed overhang, Victorian door and window surrounds, and unusual paneled door. Camelback refers to the two-story rear section of the house, not unusual in shotguns.

Simple two-bay shotgun with bracketed overhang, very plain door and window surrounds, and corner quoins.

Italianate two-bay shotgun house with bracketed overhang and corner quoins. Note the very common full-length window opening.

This is a difficult one to categorize. It has some Creole cottage features, i.e. the canted end-gabled roof, typical large dormer and chimney on end wall. However, two-bay Creole cottages are rare. Its width is that of a single shotgun house. That's really what it is.

Hip roofed two-bay shotgun house, with bracketed overhang, Italianate -Victorian window and door surrounds, and corner quoins. This is a good example of mixed motifs, so common in New Orleans architecture.

This three-bay galleried shotgun house sports a Greek revival facade with bracketed deep cornice and parapet, but very simple door and window surrounds, box pillars with Tuscan capitals. This is one of the eight similar houses built as a group in '"Halls Row," each with variations, to avoid looking like a development. The facades appear to be first-story duplications of typical Garden District side hall galleried townhouses, so they are definitely dressed for the occasion.

A three-bay classical revival galleried raised cottage with box pillars and Doric capitals, deep cornice with dentil molding and parapet, very simple surrounds, and typical New Orleans ironwork gallery railings. It shows no evidence of the later decorative styles, dating it earlier in the nineteenth century. It is at home in the Garden District.

A rather typical New Orleans three-bay shotgun, embellished with Italianate decorative elements including fleur-de-lis molding on the cornice and corner quoins.

Another distinctive classical revival three-bay shotgun, found at 2901 Coliseum Street. This home is similar to the eight in " Halls Row" in the Garden District. This sort of facade repeats the motifs found in the double galleried townhouses of the district, with box pillars and Doric capitals.

Another Garden District charmer, a three-bay somewhat Victorian style with scalloped molding on the cornice, typical of millwork readily available at the time. Otherwise it's simply dressed, and trying to look like one of the more elaborate townhouses in the area.

This three-bay shotgun at 2321 Coliseum Street appears to be the offspring of a double galleried Italianate townhouse, with its bracketed deep cornice, parapet, arched openings, and transom. The house is one of the Hall's Row group of eight, with a different and distinctive Renaissance arched gallery of larger Garden District houses.

Another Greek revival three-bay shotgun house in the lineup of the" Halls Row" eight, with simple but elegant trims. This is a small, one-story version of a large, double-galleried, side-hall townhouse prevalent in the area with typical deep cornice. This was one of the eight similar houses designed by Henry Howard and built in the 2300 block of Coliseum Street in 1868. Starr notes that for some mysterious reason they were referred to as the "seven sisters." They vary from Greek revival to Italianate in their façade styles, so as not to appear like a "development." They mirror the elegance and grandeur of the mansions in the area, appearing like their offspring. They look very much like the first story of many of the townhouses in the Garden District and Lower Garden District.)

This three-bay Italianate shotgun at 2309 Coliseum is almost a duplicate of one of its eight neighbors on the block, "Hall's Row, " with slightly different style window and door surrounds and a different transom, double bracketed cornice with low parapet, and distinctive Italianate Renaissance openings.

A more sombre looking, widened classic revival, galleried, three-bay shotgun with box pillars and simple cornice and door surrounds. It was probably built quite late, late nineteenth or early twentienh century, as the facade openings are, atypically, irregularly spaced.

Italianate three-bay Garden District type shotgun with bracketed cornice, parapet, and simple door and window treatments, with a bit of color added. This is another variation of the eight houses in "Hall's Row."

A four-bay shotgun house with saw-tooth millwork moldings on the cornice and overhang, has an otherwise simple facade. The ironwork was a later decorative addition, as this sort of item became available.

This hip roof, four-bay modified classic revival galleried shotgun is clearly of the Lower Garden District ilk, and is dressed for the occasion. It is simple, elegant, and a bit colorful, with simple narrow box pillars and only a soupcon of decorative mbellishments. Sequential arched windows suggest the late 19th century.

This Victorian galleried four-bay shotgun has a minimum of decorations except for the jig-sawed verge boards under the fish-scale shingled gable ends, offering a bit of individuality to this colorful example of the genus. The window in the gable is unusual, probably home-designed. It is also unusual to have only three supporting, turned collonettes in the gallery.

This is a charming example of an end-gabled double Creole cottage with double dormers and Italianate brackets under the canted overhang. The window and overhang cornices were probably added later. The dormers date this house early in the nineteenth century

A four-bay shotgun has minimal decorations, save the fleur-de-lis millwork molding under the cornice. There are signs of a gothic touch in the gable window.

Another Lower Garden District variety of classic revival, four-bay shotgun house with cornice and parapet, simple box columns and surrounds. This house was probably built quite early in the nineteenth century and has none of the popular decorative embellishments that came along later.

This very Victorian double shotgun house is rich with the typical manufactured millwork readily available towards the end of the nineteenth century and seen all over the city as well as the rest of the country--- a consequence of the advent of rail travel. The fish scale shingles in the gable also suggest 1880-1890.

This four-bay shotgun house may have originally been a Creole cottage, modified with a shingled front gable with Victorian window, as the more Creole end gables are visible. The vertical-boarded shutters are also characteristic of Creole cottage. This happened to many Creole cottages over the years as tastes and fashions changed.

A beautiful example of a hip-roofed, double shotgun house with Italianate brack-eted and scalloped overhang, and balustraded porch. One can't tell whether this is a double or single now, though the centered step entrance suggests the latter.

Another of the ubiquitous New Orleans double shotgun houses with simple, minimal, mostly Italianate decorative elements and a nice two-toned paint job. Although one might suspect that the bright colors on some of these shotguns is a modern touch, it's not so. These colors were in vogue all over New Orleans in the nineteenth century

In the Lower Garden district, this impressive, classic revival double shotgun house features Italianate decorations on the deep cornice, low parapet, and box pillars with Doric capitals. Houses of this type were built around Civil War times for workers' quarters.

A double shotgun house with almost no added decorative elements stands on its own with simple dignity, like a lot of these minimal domestic housing units. This one fronts on the street, has attic vents, a central chimney, and appears to be stucco over brick. It may have been a Creole cottage at one time.

Another classic, rather simple double shotgun house with little to distinguish itself from a thousand others of its ilk other than the corner quoins and fish scale shingles in the gable.

Now here's a busy, dressed-up, double shotgun Victorian lady sporting some Italianate fashions: brackets, millwork, extra mini-gables decorated with sunburst motif, and triple lights under the main gable, and an apparent bustle. This house is a camelback, with a two-story addition in back. It is an unusual color, and probably not the original. Although many of these houses were painted with a variety of wild colors, this paint job is more modern and of the sophisticated designer ilk.

Another charming Creole cottage in the Creole faubourg area, as evidenced by the end-gabled roof and six-over-six dormers. Victorian millwork added to the dormers and the double scalloping under the bracketed overhang are common later embellishments, often added to early houses.

In the Lower Garden District (or uptown) this simple double shotgun house has little of no decorative embellishments; it just looks Lower Garden District.

This Lower Garden District variety (also seen uptown) of double shotgun is closest to Italianate in style with the long bracketed overhand, deep cornices over the windows, Victorian doors, and lots of dignity and elegance. The brickwork is modern.

A double shotgun house has an Italianate motif with fleur-de-lis decorations on cornice and eaves. There is a sunburst decoration in the gable.

A double shotgun house features a bracketed overhang and simple classic surrounds. Though the transoms look Victorian, the multi-paned doors and windows are modern. It has been modernized for commercial use.

Double shotgun house with Italianate bracketed overhang and classic revival window and door surrounds.

41

A double shotgun house in Italianate-Victorian style with dramatic coloring, distinctive double brackets under the overhang, and painted quoins is a stand-out. It features lots decorative verge board, fleur-de-lis millwork under the overhang, and decorative window and door surrounds. The unusual shingles indicate that this is probably not the original gable.

This hip-roofed double shotgun is very similar to the house above, except for its lack of gable and its more modest paint job. Many shotguns were duplicates of other houses in the neighborhood, copycats, as they were called.

This double shotgun is dressed with mostly Victorian decorations: slender turned posts, a fish-scale shingled gable, and unique square stained glass lights and a stained glass transom over the door. Intricate millwork on the spandrels and gallery decorations are typical of manufactured decorative elements available on the mass market. The corner quoins are common in New Orleans.

A double shotgun with has Victorian-Queen Anne millwork and turned posts and an Italianate motif on the gallery. Otherwise it is quite typical of many others.

This simple hip-roofed double shotgun has no defining stylish motif. It is probably very early with no attempt to update with later fashions, and is almost as simple as possible except for the two-color paint job. The hanging flowerpots are one-of-a kind. The cast iron railings in the windows are later additions for security

A rather busily decorated double shotgun in the Italianate manner with brackets, cornices, pilasters, and entablature. Compare this attempt to decorate with going fashions to the previous home above's simplicity.

A rather standard early twentieth century uptown shotgun has mostly Victorian styling. The windowed dormer, transom, and top window panes are colored glass. The clapboards are thin. Its style is reminiscent of many homes throughout the country built at that time.

An elegant and dignified Lower Garden District classic revival double shotgun with heavy bracketed and modillioned cornice, box pillars, Doric capitals and heavy window and door cornices, is typical of Civil War era workers housing.

This quietly elegant four-bay Creole cottage has a plastered facade. The side walls are probably flat cypress timbers. The four window and door openings are identical, with thin, squared, recessed surrounds, typical of early plastered Creole cottages. The louvered closures seen here are probably a later modification, as Creole doors were usually vertical planks and hung with heavy metal hinges. The end-gabled roof is slightly cantered. The dormers are also typical of an earlier period, with their round-headed six-over-six paned lights flanked by fluted pilasters.

A five-bay double shotgun house has Victorian millwork in the gallery, slender turned columns and little else to distinguish it from many others of its ilk except for the unusual five-bay conformation. Probably early twentieth century

A Greek revival raised center hall cottage (sometimes referred to as plantation style villa) has a double row of dentils on the deep cornice, fluted Greek columns with Corinthian capitals, elegant door treatment with box pilasters and dentiled cornice. This is a popular style, with many just like it in the Garden District and Lower Garden District.

This classic revival center hall style plantation villa is simple in design and lacking any decorative elements save for the door surround with transom and side lights. This one is atypically low to the ground.

A Greek revival raised center hall house has a bracketed and dentiled cornice topped with a low parapet, and fluted columns with Corinthian capitals. The recessed door has a transom and sidelights, and both the door and window surrounds are heavily corniced. The entablature with dentiled cornice and architrave. The obviously very high ceilings were a must in semi-tropical New Orleans weather. There are many of these center hall houses in the Garden District, an American contribution to New Orleans architecture.

Classic revival raised plantation style cottage with square columns capped by simple capitals. This double house has Greek details on the door and window surrounds. The brick lower level and steps indicate that this house was renovated for rental use.

A plain, hip-roofed five-bay Italianate cottage is dressed in good taste. This could have been a double shotgun house altered to make a center hall house.

Here is another variation of the raised (plantation style) center hall cottage or villa featuring a simple design that includes bracketed and dentiled cornice and box pillars. Transom and side-lights in the door surround with pilasters were common.

A classic or Greek revival plantation style raised cottage has bracketed cornice, a row of dentils, a tiny lighted dormer, box pillars, and rather simple window and door surrounds.

An especially elegant center hall, plantation style, Italianate raised cottage (or villa) features dentils and parapet on cornice, box pillars, and Ionic capitals. The elaborately detailed door treatment with fluted pilasters, transom light, sidelights and entablature under row of dentils make this house right at home in the Garden District.

A Victorian (or Queen Anne) extended three-bay house has slender double columns. The window lights and transom are typical in a Queen Anne, though the parapet with lights and decorative balustrades is uncommon.

A raised classic revival center hall Louisiana cottage has a pilastered dormer with double arched windows topped by keystones and carved detailing in its gable. The pediment contains detailed carvings and fluted eaves. Other distinguishing features include a bracketed roof cornice, box pillars with Ionic capitals, an interesting fan shaped transom over lighted door and sidelights, Italianate pediments over the windows, and iron railings on the roofline. This classic Louisiana house style is sometimes referred to as an American Cottage.

A Greek revival center hall raised cottage (or villa style) at 1435 Jackson Avenue hias a high, Italianate dormer with pilasters and double arched windows. The house was built in 1883 by architect William Fitzner. The overhang is modestly bracketed and treated with dentil molding, and the fluted Greek columns have Corinthian capitals. This American Cottage style was popular until the end of the nineteenth century, and was a very common New Orleans variety of domestic architecture.

Another double galleried side hall townhouse with nothing unusual as decorations: Corinthian capital crown columns on both stories underscored by ironwork railings.

A Greek revival double galleried townhouse is capped by a dentiled cornice atop box pillars with ionic capitals. Simple squared window and door surrounds sit recessed in galleries dressed up by the usual ironwork railings. This style was very popular in New Orleans and often lined the streets one after the other to make a very impressive scene.

A very popular Greek revival double galleried side hall townhouse has box pillars, classic revival window and door surrounds, and a simple roof cornice with para- pet. There are practically no other decorative elements except for the usual ornate cast ironwork railings. Another example of an ubiquitous New Orleans house style, most probably mid-nineteenth century.

A dignified New Orleans signature dwelling, as seen all over the Lower Garden District, is a Greek revival double galleried side hall townhouse with fluted columns and Corinthian capitals, simple window cornices, classic revival door surround, and cast iron railings.

A Greek revival townhouse has a two-level gallery with box pillars topped by Doric capitals. Many houses in New Orleans are almost identical to this one, with its bracketed and dentiled cornice, low parapet, and Italianate cornices over door and windows.

They just loved parapets in New Orleans! This Greek revival side hall double galleried townhouse has unusual split fluted box pillars and Doric capitals. The dentiled cornice with two windows in parapet is an unusual design.

54

This Greek revival center hall galleried townhouse has dentiled and bracketed cornice, box pillars, and Doric capitals, but is otherwise quite simple and unadorned.

The unusual black door of is surrounded with sidelights and an arched transom, recessed behind a simple square framed entrance with a fluted pilaster on one side.

One of the more impressive Greek revival townhouses with side additions, this one has dentiled and bracketed cornice with parapet, split fluted columns and Corinthian capitals. It is a most elegant and outstanding example of a Garden District mansion.

A classical revival side hall house in the Lower Garden District has an Italianate motif. Box pillars support the two-level galleries. Window and door surrounds are Italianate-Victorian. The home is nicely painted, with quoins both on corners and between openings.

A two and a half story Italianate townhouse is very New Orleans, with both balcony and gallery. A variety of brackets were used up and down, and carved spandrels form arched porch openings between box pillars. The decorative elements are mostly Italianate, including brackets under the overhanging half-storey which has horizontal windows with carvings in between. This is a typical Lower Garden District townhouse.

An Italianate townhouse is almost identical to the previous house, but without the gallery or balcony. Both were probably done by the same builder, with modifications for each owner. It was common in New Orleans to copy an existing house rather than call on an architect.

These attached townhouses show elements of both Victorian and Italianate motifs. The slender turned pillars and millwork borders are Victorian whereas the window treatments are more Italianate. It is another example of how in New Orleans builders often freely mixed styles to suit their fancy and utilized the manufactured millwork available at the time. In many cases, houses would start out in one style and later, as fashions changed, more contemporary motifs were added. This one is quite unique.

Another of the attached New Orleans townhouses with mostly Italianate decorative elements: a bracketed and scalloped overhang and essentially Italianate window and door surrounds, plus corner quoins.

A typical New Orleans garden, commonly found behind any townhouse.

A typical rear garden as seen all over New Orleans, gracing anything from a shotgun to a fancy townhouse. One can't tell by the view from the street what sort of beautiful garden area lurks behind.

This one-of-a-kind six-bayed saddleback is a rather non-descript specimen, with unusual segmented arches in the center and multiple door and widow openings. It is most likely a two-family residence. The decorations are Victorian style.

Basically a square colonial surrounded by double porches, this style is frequently seen in tropical climes but not that much in New Orleans. It is quite plain except for the Ionic columns.

A side addition breaks the symmetry of a Greek revival townhouse featuring dentils and modillions under cornice topped by a prominent parapet. The fluted columns are topped by Corinthian capitals on the second floor and Ionic on the first. The home is typical of those found in the Lower Garden District.

This New Orleans "Creole" townhouse has Italianate decorative elements including a bracketed and scalloped cornice, arched window openings and recessed door behind Italianate door surround with keystone. This townhouse is in an area of shotgun houses, the Creole faubourgs. It's kind of a two-story five-bay shotgun townhouse: not unusual in New Orleans.

A two-family townhouse with classical revival and Italianate elements features a narrow pillared gallery downstairs and balcony upstairs with ironwork railings. It's sort of a maverick, with mixed features probably individually designed and custom built like many others in New Orleans, but reflecting the more formal prevalent styles.

(Opposite Page)
This specimen should be called the Hodge-Podge House, with its variety of decorative styles and elements. There is a lower level gallery with balcony above. The cornice over first floor overhang has dentils, whereas the upper cornice is bracketed with two different type brackets. The gabled roof contains a carved decorated pediment above four openings, louvered and plain under another bracketed cornice. The arched windows are topped with keystone decorations on both levels. The columns are fluted with Corinthian capitals. And there are quoins on the corners. This is a really dressed -up Victorian lady.

61

This Victorian-Queen Anne has a multi-faceted mixture of styles, surfaces, and openings. Located on Esplanade Road, it sports a sampling of just about every style of architecture described thus far: Greek Revival columns and capitals, Italianate brackets, dormer and arched openings, and Queen Anne towers and turrets,. With all that, it's not as graceful or appealing as most of New Orleans houses.

The Plantations

Inasmuch as much of New Orleans' expansion in the early part of the nineteenth century came as a result of the subdividing of large plantation parcels whose owners sold them off for a variety of reasons. The lots were mostly bought by *gens de colour libre* , the major new group to arrive in New Orleans. They were often builders themselves and proceeded to build their own homes. As a consequence, most of the plantations houses have been destroyed, leaving only a very few close to the city. Of those remaining within a few miles, the following four provide a look at what kind of plantation buildings was around earlier. Each plantation acreage was then designated as a foubourg and named after the previus plantation owner, i.e the fourbourg Maringy. The presence of the following plantations is in order to emphasize the Greek temple architecture that became so popular in southern plantation architecture and led to the style being incorporated into more modest dwellings in New Orleans and other southern cities.

Houmas plantation, not far from New Orleans, was also spared the usual sacrifice for developments of lower income housing. This white columned mansion in the Greek Revival style is a good example of the typical Louisiana plantation manor house that surrounded New Orleans before the great expansion of the city limits. It is surrounded on three sides by galleries and fourteen Doric columns and capitals. It has a hipped roof topped by a glass-enclosed belvedere and there are two dormers on each of three sides. It has been the scene of many Hollywood movies, as it typifies the Louisiana Plantation House and has been meticulously restored to its original condition. It lies on the Mississippi near Burnside, in Ascension Parish.

Greenwood Plantation, built in 1830 in West Feleciana Parish, exhibits the owner's attempt to duplicate the Greek Parthenon, even using the same eight columns on the gallery. It was used in the Civil War as a hospital. In 1960 it was burned to the ground after being struck by lightning, and underwent a complete reconstruction over a period of twelve years. It is one of many enormous and impressive plantations built along the Mississippi as one after another plantation owner became enamored of and celebrated the Greek Revival movement. It became the most obvious, effective, and universally accepted status symbol in the area.

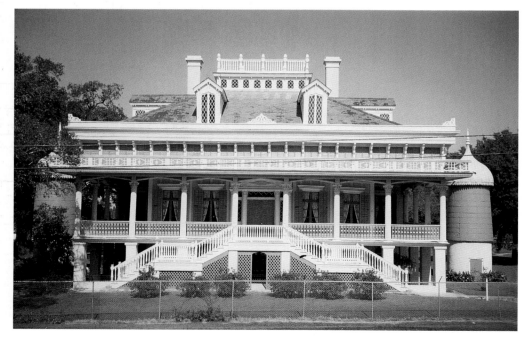

San Francisco is a strikingly unusual plantation house located in Reserve, about twenty miles west of New Orleans. Built in 1856, this stunning house is added mostly for its striking visual appeal as an interesting addition to a book of New Orleans house photographs. In a total departure from the usual plantation edifice, this architectural potpourri combines elements of the Victorian, Classic Revival, and Gothic styles to form what the original owner, Edmond Bozonier Marmillon, hoped would resemble a Mississippi steamboat. He succeeded in building a strikingly ornate and altogether unique mansion like no other along the Mississippi. The mansion was acquired in 1975 by an oil company, which has restored it to its original grandeur, furnished it in the elaborate style of the 1850s and opened it to the public for an admission fee.

The Garden District

The Garden District of New Orleans, like Fifth Avenue in New York City or Beacon Hill in Boston, became the exclusive suburb of New Orleans in the Nineteenth Century. The growing economy of New Orleans in the early 1800s created considerable wealth, which was largely in the hands of Anglo-Saxon, self-made men. Their fortunes came from cotton, tobacco, and banking, the latter with lucrative connections to New York City. A society of elite movers and shakers developed and, as is the usual trend, were wont to associate with their own kind. Looking for a place where they could live, socialize, and feel at home with others of like mind, they found a suburban location about two miles west of the center of New Orleans. The Garden District was laid out formally in 1820 and serious building commenced by 1830. There followed the development of a neighborhood of elaborate, elegant, and distinctive mansions.

The profession of architecture was just appearing in the United States around 1820, and in the next two decades accomplished architects were arriving in the area to cater to the desires and whims of the affluent gentry interested in locating in the newly developed area. Most of these architects arrived from the British Isles. They brought with them the London Townhouse, which became popular in the Garden District and Lower Garden District.

Of the early New Orleans architects of the Garden District, the most prominent were Henry Howard and Lewis E. Reynolds. They were described by Starr as "the architects of opulence" who created "outstanding and enduring monuments" of New Orleans architecture. There were others, most notably the Galliers, Sr., and Jr., emigrants from Ireland, who left an architectural legacy in their own distinctive styles. The early group also included Thomas Wharton and John Turpin, from England, and Sam Johnson from Scotland. The only local boy was William E. Freret, a native of New Orleans. Albert Diettel and Edward Gottheil came from Germany. Works of all of these designers and builders are presented in the following group of Garden District houses.

In the beginning, the Greek Revival was the architectural style of choice in the Garden District. It was the most popular style in the rest of the country at that time. Although it began to decline in popularity in the rest of country in the 1840s in favor of other styles, such as the Italianate , Victorian and Second Empire, it continued to be the style of choice in New Orleans well into the latter part of the century. Greek Revival stylistic expression was ubiquitous in all the major house plans. Starr notes that, "After 1852, a growing uniformity made itself felt. Its three basic components were the raised cottage, the three-bay London plan dwelling, and the five bay center-hall house. All three featured galleries or verandas and all three gravitated towards the same basic types of columns."[11] They were dominated by Greek Revival elements, such as entablature, cornices, parapets, the three Greek type columns and capitals and Greek-key door and window surrounds.

However, as the newer styles became popular in the rest of the country, they appeared in New Orleans mostly in the form of renovations and additions to existing homes. Italianate embellishments and decorations became *de riguer* in fancy Garden District homes. Supply houses began producing a variety of decorative elements, such as brackets, cornices, door frames, and other fittings in the Italianate style, The result was that the facades of many Garden District houses had an Italianate facelift, as evidence of their owners' and builders' architectural sophistication.

Less popular, but in evidence, were the Victorian and Second Empire decorations. This accounts for the fact that many houses in the Garden District exhibit a variety of stylistic elements making for a mixture of architectural styles in the same building. Most Garden District homes defy description by any one distinct architectural style. The Italianate predominated, however, and was considered the *sine qua non* by New Orleans builders for renovations. Almost everyone wanted Italianate brackets under the eaves of their homes, so they became ubiquitous in the Garden District and were vigorously produced by all the supply houses.

The other architectural renovation popular in New Orleans was cast iron work, from fences and gates around the property to elaborate two-story galleries. Cast iron decorations were introduced in the area in the 1840s and 50s, most of which came from northeastern foundries. However, demand was so great that New Orleans boiler-making foundries began manufacturing ornate cast iron work. As Starr notes, "It was the custom designed and specially manufactured two story galleries that had the greatest impact on Garden District Architecture."[11] Undoubtedly, they have become a unique and almost universal symbol of New Orleans. Cast iron work became immensely popular after the Civil War, as foundries could then turn their attention to peaceful production.

The following collection represents a sampling of the remaining well-known mansion-size houses in the Garden District.

The Hibson-Haach House, 1224 Jackson Avenue, was built in 1860, and designed by the well-known New Orleans architect, Henry Howard. This classical revival bay-windowed plantation style center hall raised cottage has a deep cornice decorated with dentils and brackets. The recessed door is surrounded by pilasters and dentiled cornice. Fluted columns with Corinthian capitals and ironwork railing with lyres and flower designs decorate the gallery. Ironwork designs were usually individualized and custom made.

The Dominique Stella House at 2915 Chestnut Street was designed by Frederick Wing. This Greek revival side hall townhouse has two pillared galleries, with Greek fluted columns and Corinthian capitals upstairs and box columns and Doric capitals down. The dominant decorative style is Italianate. The double-bracketed cornice is decorated with unusual dentils, scalloped millwork and a low parapet. The arched transom light is distinctive, capping sidelights and a pilaster door surround. Ironwork railings adorn the upper gallery.

The Morris-Israel-Aron House at 1331 First Street typifies New Orleans style. It was designed and built by Samuel Jamison and James McIntosh beginning in 1860, but construction was delayed by the Civil War. It wasn't finished until1868. It is embellished with ornate cast iron work in railings, spandrels, and tracers. These galleries were manufactured and installed by a local foundry owned by Jacob Baumiller, who made mostly steam boilers up to that time, producing the first architectural ironwork in New Orleans as demand increased dramatically. Ironwork decorations were to become a defining element in New Orleans architecture and are universally associated with the city.

The Lewis Elkins House, 1410 Second Street, was built in 1858-59 as a Greek revival mansion with Corinthian columns, but was later renovated to look more Italianate as that style became fashionable. Italianate pediment over the arched windows figured in the redo. This kind of change in architectural styles was very common in New Orleans making houses quite individual and un-conventional, and often difficult to describe architecturally

The Carroll-Brown (or Crawford) House at 1315 First Street is a lavishly decorated stuccoed brick New Orleans mansion. Designed by Samuel Jameson and built in 1869, it is mostly Italianate in style with an extensive ironwork gallery structure attached to the facade at a later date. The ironwork pillars, railings, brackets, spandrels, and decorative lacework borders make for a typical New Orleans architectural specimen. Arched window and door surrounds are unique, with Italianate pediments downstairs giving this mansion a rather *grand dame* appearance. It is topped by a heavy, modillioned cornice and the very decorative parapet. This is truly a New Orleans *grande maison.*

Sweet-Uhalt House at 1236 Jackson Street was designed by the well-known New Orleans architect Henry Howard, and built by Frederick Wing between 1874-76. This was Howard's first Victorian mansion to which he added some Italianate embellishments, i.e. the multi-bracketed cornice and overhang, the balcony surrounding the front of the house, and the galleried first floor. Unique chamfered square wooden pillars hold up the decorated cornice and arched segmental openings. Note the unusual Italianate window on the wing. The window pediments are mostly Italianate, also.

The Joseph Merrick Jones House, 2425 Coliseum Street, was built in 1850. This Greek revival mansion has double split box pillars on the two level galleries that front the entire house. Heavy, double-bracketed cornice and plain window and door surrounds make this house hard to fit into any particular architectural style, but that is not unusual in New Orleans and this grand house is right at home here.

This lovely Italianate mansion is loaded with heavy Italianate brackets in the usual places, and then some. Note those on the Queen Anne bay- windows. The box pillars have one large, dressy flute, which gives a formal look to the house. This is truly a mixed motif gem!

This house at 2594 Prytania Street serves as home to the New Orleans Opera Association, Womens' Guild. It is a striking example of mixed architecture. The typical Greek revival two-level townhouse section, built in 1858, was a frequent sight in New Orleans, with its dentiled cornice topped with a pedimented dormer, fluted columns with both Coriinthian (upstairs) and Doric (downstairs) capitals. A rather typical Queen Anne octagonal tower, a design popular in the 1880s and '90s, was added at a later date. Dr. and Mrs. Bacchelle Seebold restored the house and willed it to the Womens' Guild in 1966.

Toby's Corner at 2340 Prytania Street, on the corner of First Street, is said to be the oldest house in the Garden District. It was built by Tom Toby in 1838 on the edge of the Livandais Plantation. This large plantation house was built on brick piers in the style of West Indies plantations. Tom Toby made his fortune as a wheelright.

The Beauregard House, built in 1826, was named for Pierre Gustave Toutant Beauregard, who lived here following his return from the Civil War. It served as a boarding house during the war, and for a while was occupied by the Swiss Consul. Early in the twentieth century it deteriorated and was almost demolished before being saved by locals interested in its restoration. In 1944, Francis Parkington Keyes, the author, purchased the house for her own use, and began its restoration. She eventually turned the house over to a philanthropic organization and it is presently a museum open to the public.

Built by William Buckner in 1858, this beautiful large Greek revival center hall mansion at 2507 Jackson Avenue functioned as the Buckner College until 1920, when it was occupied by Soale College, a business school, until the 1980s.

The Pritchard-Pigott House is a Greek revival center hall mansion designed by Howard and Diettel. It was built in1858 with mammoth full height fluted columns and ionic capitals. This one looks like it is trying to imitate the stately plantation houses of the Mississippi River collection, yet is small enough to fit in the city. It was renovated in 1909, giving it a Renaissance revival appearance by architects Soule and Mac Donnell.

The Bradish Johnson House at 2343 Prytnia Street, was attributed to James Freret by one author. However, Starr claims this is a mis-attribution, and was actually designed by Lewis Reynolds. (Some people claim that Reynolds has suffered a number of mis-attributions in the Garden District.) It is a striking example of the French Ecole des Beaux Arts school of architecture. It's an elaborate, enormous, multi-galleried facade, variously decorated with lots of Italianate bracketing and dentiling. As Starr notes, it was "ornamented with virtually every stylistic feature pioneered by Napoleon's architects in Paris." Barely visible is what looks like a "widow's walk" roof area surrounded by ornate ironwork railings. Corinthian columns and capitals on the lower level adds a Greek revival touch. Whoever designed this one had a really good time and spared no expense or stretch of imagination. Since 1929 it has been occupied by the McGehee School.

The Robinson House at 1415 3rd Street, in the heart of the Garden
District, was designed, allegedly, by the famous New Orleans architect, James Gallier, Jr. Starr claims
that this is another mis-attribution of one of Lewis Reynold's houses. He states," nearly all of Reynold's finest works came to be attributed erroneously to James Galliert Sr." Built in 1864 as a standard
center hall colonial, the Italianate gallery with unusual curved ends was added in 1870. The house is
of large proportions, with 15-1/2 foot ceilings and ornate ironwork on the sides. It stands out even
in New Orleans as a striking architectual specimen. In New Orleans you *had* to have a parapet, it
was *de rigeur* for any fashion-conscious homeowner. The design of this house is truly one-of-a-kind
anywhere--especially the curved ends of the facade. The delicate, extensive lace-like ornamental
ironwork covering one side of the house stands out as unusual even in New Orleans. The other side
of the house has elaborate stable buildings, described by Starr as "these modest but elegant ap-
pendages are among the most perfect buildings from New Orleans' golden age."

The Robinson House has a recessed door with double arched Italianate lights and clear transom. The impressive door surround includes beautiful fluted pilasters topped by ornate Italianate entablature with a low-arched opening and heavy cornice. It can only be described as Greek Revival-Italianate-Victorian.

The gate and railings of the Robinson House.

Another angle on the detailed cast iron decorative work on the Robinson House galleries.

The Robinson House, with its intricate uniquely New Orleans cast iron work,
is like nowhere else in town, or anywhere else, for that matter.

Glossary

architrave: lowest molding above columns in entablature

bay: vertical section of exterior wall containing one door or window

balustrade: vertical elements under railings

bracket: decorative ornament supporting roof overhang in Italianate houses

chamfered pillars; box pillars with concave vertical cutout on edges

camelback house: has two-story addition to rear of shotgun house

capital: decorative ornament atop Greek or Roman Revival columns

collonette: narrow, usually turned supporting gallery column

cornice: the band of plain molding under the roofline in classic and Greek revival houses

Corinthian: gracefully elaborate order of classical Greek or Roman architecture

Creole: early inhabitants of Louisiana of mixed European, Caribbean and African origin along with Acadians from French Canada. Often used to describe anyone or anything of Louisiana or New Orleans. origin: native Louisianians. Loosely denoting anything associated with New Orleans and its environs

Doric: classical order of Greek or Roman architecture, characterized by simplicity

double shotgun house: A pair of attached two-bay shotgun houses with a common wall

dentils: square-shaped decorative elements equally spaced under roofline

Eastlake style: Excessively ornate architectural style, similar to Victorian, named after furniture designer, Charles Eastlake.

entablature: decorative area below roofline in classic and Greek revival houses, including cornice, frieze, and architrave

faubourg: neighborhood (or section of city) originally a plantation which had been subdivided into building lots, named after the plantation or its owner

fluted: trimmed with parallel vertical grooves on columns and pilasters

frieze: the band of molding above the cornice in classic and Greek revival houses

gallery: front porch of classic revival townhouse, usually double, upstairs and down.

gothic: decorative style characterized by arched window shapes and architectural structures

Greek Revival [[NOTE: needs definition]]

hip roof: low pyramidal shaped roof, characteristic of Creole cottages, often referred to as maisonettes

Ionic: classical order of Greek or Roman architecture characterized by ornamental scrolls (spiral volutes)

Italianate: decorative style popular in the 1880s-90s, characterized by heavy roof overhangs, bracketing, deep cornices and turrets

maison de maitre: early Creole galleried hall-less house of two to four rooms

mansard roof: flattop roof with roofing on slanted upper storywall.

modillions: refined large dentil-like ornaments

overhang: pronounced roofline protruding over facade, usually in Italianate houses

parapet: decorative pediment type extension above the cornice in a Greek revival house

pediment: decorative element above cornice in roof or in door surround

pilaster: vertical decorative element of door surround

Queen Anne: a variety of Victorian style characterized by multi-faced walls, very ornate details, and odd shaped extra bays, dormers, and towers

quoins: Italianate faux-stone corner decoration

raised cottage: house in which main living floor is raised on foundation a full story above ground.

segmental opening: section of facade between columns

shotgun house: so-named because a shot through the front door would not hit any wall until the rear wall, i.e either a long hallway or series of rooms with doors in a line. Popular in the Caribbean, later in Louisiana, and especially New Orleans

sidelight: vertical series of window panes in door surround

spandrel: decorative element in angle between column and roofline

transom: decorative window panes above doors

verge boards: Decorative molding under eaves in Victorian houses, usually jig-sawed lace-like woodworking.

Victorian: architectural style and decorative elements popular in the latter part of Nineteenth Century characterized by very detailed and excessively ornate elements, lots of turned and jig-sawed woodwork.

Endnotes

[1]Gamble, Robert, *Historic Architecture in Alabama: A Primer of Styles and Types.* 1810-1930. Tuscaloosa, Alabama University of Alabama Press, 1990

[2]Toledano, R., Evans, S., Christovich, M. L. *New Orleans Architecture, Vol. IV , The Creole Suburbs,* New Orleans, Pelican Publishing Company, 1974. Page 54

[3]Caemmerer, Alex., *The Houses of Key West,* Sarasota, Pineapple Press, 1992

[4]Toledano, Roulhac, B et al. *New Orleans Architecture, Vol. IV , The Creole Suburbs* New Orleans, Pelican Publishing Company, 1974. Page 72

[5]Vlach, John Michael. *Sources of the Shotgun House: African and Caribbean Antecedents for Afro-American Architecture* PhD Thesis, Indiana University, 1975

[6]Toledano, Roulhac, B et al. *New Orleans Architecture, Vol. IV , The Creole Suburbs* New Orleans, Pelican Publishing Company, 1972. Page 71

[7]Cultural Survey of Key West, Florida

[8]Christovich, Mary Louise, Toledano, et al,. *New Orleans Architecture, Vol I, The Lower Garden District.* New Orleans, Pelican Publishing Company, 1971, Page 43

[9]Ibid. Page 48

[10]Ibid. Page 55

[11]Starr, S, Frederick, " Southern Comfort, the Garden District of New Orleans:" , Princeton Architectural Press, NYC.

Further Reference Reading

Malone, Paul and Lee, *The Majesty of the Garden District*, Pelican Publishing, Gretna La.
Vogt, Lloyd, *New Orleans Houses*, Pelican Publishing 2003, Gretna La.